Jack's Stories

Inspirational Stories for the Soul

Jack Rogers

Jack's Stories
Published by Yawn's Publishing
2555 Marietta Hwy, Ste 103
Canton, GA 30114
www.yawnspublishing.com

Library of Congress Control Number: 2020906848

ISBN13: 978-1-947773-75-2

Printed in the United States

All quoted scripture is taken from the King James Version.

Contents

Story One

Getting to Heaven with a 70

My wife and I, along with our two young sons, moved to LaGrange, Georgia in 1972. I was a math teacher, football, basketball and baseball coach.

In 1980, I was named Athletic Director at LaGrange High School and later, Assistant Principal at the Jr High School. When I moved to LaGrange in 1972, our head coach and Athletic Director had just retired. He lived right across the street from the school and visited us almost every day for the seventeen years that we lived in LaGrange. He was quite a character. One day we were, strangely enough, talking about spiritual things and he made the comment, "I just want to get into Heaven with a 70". Now you would have to know him to understand that comment. He had a super wife and three great children. In fact, his oldest son was my dentist. However, he had a reputation as a heavy drinker and quite a party person especially at coaching clinics.

His comment, "I just want to get into Heaven with a 70" has stuck with me for more than twenty years.

For the first few years, I took a very arrogant approach. I told myself, "Well I don't drink or smoke and I'm certainly not a party animal. I have never cheated on my wife. I go to church every Sunday that I'm in town. I taught a sixth grade Sunday School class for a couple of years and alternated teaching our adult Sunday School class. Man, if Coach can get a 70, I ought to at least get an 85 or 90." Then about twenty years ago I decided to read the Bible from cover to cover. I read one chapter every night for two-and-one-half years. I said, "Surely I'm up to about a 92 or 93 now."

Then my second phase began. I looked around at spiritual leaders in LaGrange and Rome. I read that one is supposed to tithe and anything over one tenth is a gift. I read that we are asked to be humble and become a servant to others. Pray intently, praise God, and don't judge or condemn others. That didn't sound like me at all. If they are a 95, surely I'm not over a 25 or 30. I'm not going to make it. As far as getting to heaven, I'm a failure. I'm just not going to make it.

Then, I took three Disciple Bible courses (I, II, IV) and learned that we don't get to heaven by our own good works, but only by God's grace and our salvation.

In Ephesians 2:4-5, Paul says,
4 But God, who is rich in mercy, for his great love wherewith he loved us,
5 Even when we were dead in sins, hath quickened us together with Christ, (by grace ye are saved).

We are saved, not because we make a 70, 80 or 90, but only because of God's grace and salvation.

What is salvation? John Wesley, founder of the Methodist Church said the following, "It is not a blessing which lies on the other side of death...it is a present thing...it is the entire work of God, from the first dawning of grace in the soul till it is consummated in glory".

Wesley was convinced that the affliction of sin resulted in more than guilt and the need for forgiveness. The debilitating nature of sin also required the healing power of God's Spirit.

Wesley described salvation as "a therapy of the soul". He stated, "By salvation I mean, not barely... deliverance from hell, or going to heaven, but a present deliverance from sin, a restoration of the soul to its primitive health, its original purity; a recovery of the divine nature; the renewal of our souls after the image of God in righteousness and true holiness".

A John Wesley scholar, Albert Outler, described Wesley's conception of justification, sanctification, and consummation (in heaven) "as a journey from the barely human, to the truly human, to the fully human".

This movement toward the fully human enables our commitment to a life of good works. We will never be good enough to be saved (or to make a 70), but neither can we be saved apart from a commitment to do good.

In Mark 1:17, And Jesus said unto them, Come ye after me, and I will make you to become fishers of men.

Within these words is an offer of God's salvation and a call to serve. And that is our call today...to serve and to do good.

Wesley did not believe that we could be good enough to be saved, but he did believe that we would never be saved unless we worked to be good.

Story 2

Life is not Fair

"Life is not fair." We've all heard this a million times. I made this statement at the opening faculty meeting to my elementary teachers at the beginning of each new school year. There was a reason. Elementary teachers have their "little darlings" with them all day long except for small periods of time when they are at Art or Music. Because of scheduling problems, some teachers might have thirty minutes of planning time a day while others may have forty-five minutes. I was always the first to hear about it. My answer was "life is not fair".

I'm an avid golfer, and we all know that golf is not fair. I may pull my drive into a tree, and it may bounce left and into the water. My competitor may pull his driver, hit the same tree and his ball may bounce out in the middle of the fairway. The golfing gods are not always "fair".

My wife, Sandra, was diagnosed with MS two months before she was to retire after thirty-two years in public education. She could easily have said, "That's not fair," but she didn't. She was just thankful that she was able to complete her long career in education before her health would not allow her to work.

Our neighbor also has MS and had to go on disability after a long career as an engineer. We visited with him and his wife shortly after Sandra's diagnosis to discuss her limitations. He told her that she would never be able to do extreme physical activity again. Sandra threw up her hands. (She has never exercised in her life.) He told Sandra that she would never be able to stay out in the heat during the summer again. Sandra threw up her hands. (She has always felt that sweating was next to sinning.) He said that she would never be able to cut the grass. Again, Sandra threw up her hands. (She has never cut a blade of grass in her life.) Sandra told him that she thought God had perfectly matched her disability with her personality.

If one person in the Old Testament had a reason to say, "Life is not fair", it was Joseph. Joseph was the eleventh of Jacob's twelve sons and the firstborn of Rachel. We know that Joseph was the favorite child of Jacob and was given a coat of many colors. We know that about the envy of his older brothers. They threw him in to a pit and planned to kill him, but his brother, Reuben, persuaded his other brothers not to. Instead of allowing him to die in the pit, they sold him to a caravan of Ishmaelites making its way to Egypt. They sold him in the slave market to an officer of Pharaoh, an Egyptian named Potiphar.

We all know the story of Potiphar's wife who made false accusations against Joseph and whose improper advances were rejected by Joseph. Joseph was cast into prison, where he remained for years.

We know that Pharaoh had two dreams that no one could interpret. God gave Joseph the ability to interpret these dreams of seven years of plenty followed by seven years of famine. Pharaoh made Joseph head of the royal granaries. As the head of the department of state, Joseph became one of the officials next in rank to the pharaoh. Joseph demonstrated noble character, gentleness, patience and a forgiving spirit.

Patience is a fruit of the Spirit. In Galatians 5:22, Paul says, *But the fruit of the Spirit is love, joy, peace, longsuffering, gentleness, goodness, faith.*

Patience is a virtue that God prizes highly and seems to be best developed under trials. In Romans 5:3-4, Paul says, *3 And not only so, but we glory in tribulations also: knowing that tribulation worketh patience.*

4 And patience, experience; and hope.

Life is not fair, but God is. God offers all of us His grace. All we have to do is accept it. Some of us may have to persevere through illness, some of us through the loss of a loved one, some through divorce or some through the loss of financial wealth. But no matter what our suffering is, God loves us all and grants us His mercy. Life will never be fair, but God's mercy will always be with us.

Let us pray,

Our Father, we thank you for your unconditional grace. Help us to persevere through whatever trials we personally face. Help us to remember that our hope lies in you.

Amen

Story 3

Adopted Cat

My wife and I have never been "pet people". When our boys were small, we did have a couple of dogs. The first was a small chihuahua that one of my wife's students gave her. One day while we were at work, a neighbor's large bulldog got out of his fenced-in area and mutilated "Fumble". Later, a large German Shepherd, named Duke after John Wayne, adopted us, and we started feeding and petting her. When we took her to get her shots, she never would let us touch her again.

Several months ago, we noticed a beautiful brown-gray and white cat hanging around our front steps and back deck. She seemed well-fed and healthy. We didn't really want a cat. My wife is allergic to all cat hair; plus, we didn't want to be tied down when we took trips. So, for about three months we ignored her and didn't feed her, assuming that she had a perma-nent home elsewhere. We began to notice more and more that our cat was never leaving our lot. She was sleeping under our house and hunting in our back-yard. We have a security light in our backyard, and we noticed her sitting on the bench on our deck at night and studying our yard for a possible food source. After about three months, I couldn't stand it anymore and started petting her. She would even sit on my lap for short periods of time. The next day we started feeding her. The following week we talked to our veterinarian and he said to bring her by his office, and he would check her out. When we did, we found out that she was not a she but a neutered male. Sandra had already named her Jack's Cat, so we just shortened the name to J.C.

I thought about the progression of J.C.'s adopting us months before we paid any attention to him. We ignored him, but he wouldn't go away. He persisted and persisted. We wouldn't feed him or nourish him. Finally, we broke down and acknowledged his existence in our lives. Now what a great loving relationship we have with J.C.

Isn't this the same relationship that we have with another J.C., not Jack's Cat, but Jesus Christ? God adopted us; He put His Spirit within us, and we became subject to His control.

In Romans 8:16-17, Paul says that,

16 The Spirit itself beareth witness with our spirit, that we are the children of God:

17 And if children, then heirs; heirs of God, and joint-heirs with Christ; if so be that we suffer with him, that we may be also glorified together.

And in Ephesians 1:4-5, Paul says,

4 According as he hath chosen us in him before the foundation of the world, that we should be holy and without blame before him in love:

5 Having predestinated us unto the adoption of children by Jesus Christ to himself, according to the good pleasure of his will,

Just as we did with our cat, J.C., we can deny the existence of Jesus Christ or, like most of us do, we can just ignore Him. He will not go away though. He persists and persists. Only when we acknowledge Him and His grace will we benefit from His loving mercy. He will feed us and nourish us and allow us to have a wonderful relationship with Him. He will change our lives as surely as our cat changed the lives of my wife and myself.

Remember that J.C. (Jesus Christ) lives under your house, on your deck, waiting to be adopted. But, like a cat, I've come to know His love is unfailing and unconditional, even when we're slow to respond.

Let us Pray,

Our Father,

Thank You for adopting us as your sons and heirs. Help us to acknowledge You and accept your grace and mercy.

Amen

Story 4

"Praise the Lord"

In Ephesians 1:6 & 12, Paul tells us that we are to be the praise of God's glory.

Ephesians 1:6, *To the praise of the glory of his grace, wherein he hath made us accepted in the beloved.*

Ephesians 1:12, *That we should be to the praise of his glory, who first trusted in Christ.*

During the middle of the 1970s, I was coaching at LaGrange High School and started a chapter of the Fellowship of Christian Athletes. For several summers I took four or five athletes to the FCA camp on Black Mountain about fifteen miles east of Asheville, NC. I always took my wife and two small boys. During the day the athletes competed in sports competition on the fields near the bottom of the mountain. At night we listened to noted college and pro-speakers and participated in small group discussions.

One week on a Tuesday morning, the FCA counselors took the sponsors' children on a rigorous climb up to the top of Black Mountain. They signed out at the camp headquarters and were to sign in when they returned before lunch. Our oldest son, Jeff, returned to the cabin about 11:30 am. About noon, three worried counselors came to our cabin to report that our youngest son, Jason, age five, had not reported in with the rest of the children and was missing somewhere on the mountain. My wife and I

11

panicked and asked if we could join the search for him. They said, "No, just wait at the cabin, that they had a search party hunting for him." My wife and I spent the longest two or three hours of our lives on our knees by the bed praying for Jason's safe return. Finally, about three o'clock, the relieved counselor returned a tired, emotional and scratched-up five-year-old to his parents.

He had gotten separated from the others on the rugged path on the way down the mountain, missed the turn to the assembly camp and continued down the rough trail near the bottom of the mountain. He was not found by the counselors, however. When the trail got near the ball fields, he heard the athletes yelling, "Praise the Lord." He couldn't see anyone through the heavy brush, but he knew they were Christian athletes. The year before, he had repeatedly heard them yell this when someone made a good play or was victorious. When he heard, "Praise the Lord," he made his way through the briars and bushes to the athletes and asked the coach to take him to his parents. My wife and I had never been so relieved in our lives. We really did "Praise the Lord" for answering our prayers.

"Praise" is probably the most often used word in the Bible. Praise fills the Book of Psalms, increasing in intensity toward the end. (Psalms 145-150) Psalms 113-118 are called the Hallel, the praises.

Praise for redemption also dominates the New Testament.

In Luke 2:13-14, *13 And suddenly there was with the angel a multitude of the heavenly host praising God, and saying, 14 Glory to God in the highest, and on earth peace, good will toward men.*

And in Revelation 19:5, *5 And a voice came out of the throne, saying, Praise our God, all ye his servants, and ye that fear him, both small and great.*

We all need to praise God more enthusiastically because we never know when our voices will reach a "lost five-year-old" or "a lost soul".

Story 5

A Bump in the Road

My wife and I were riding down Highway 27 on our way to South Alabama to visit my mother in the nursing home. I saw a sign on the highway saying, "Bump" and sure enough there was a "bump" in the road. About a month later, I was riding down the same highway and saw the same sign "Bump" and sure enough there was a "bump" in the road. Next month same sign, same bump. This got me to thinking. Isn't this what we do in our own lives? When we run into a "bump" in our lives, many times we don't fix or repair it. We just put up a sign.

We probably know some people (not just my wife) whose signs say, "I don't exercise," or better, "I don't sweat". We may erect a sign that says, "I don't wash dishes". I'm sure that nobody wears that sign.

Our sign may read, "I don't vote," because "one vote won't matter," or "I don't support charities," because the money gets misappropriated anyway.

My own personal sign reads: "Jack Rogers does not do that. I'll be a year older next month and never have done it, and don't plan on doing it in the future."

In our church life, we also put up signs – they read, "I can't teach Sunday School"; "I can't serve on a committee"; "I can't commit thirty-four weeks to a

Disciple class"; "I can't tithe"; or "I can't attend a men's prayer breakfast every Tuesday."

Let's go back to that Highway 27 sign that says, "Bump". The sign should probably read: "Get ready for a disruption in your drive. The road is uneven but there is no one who will ever take the time or trouble to fix it. Get used to it."

Because we are Christians, we know that people can change. If people cannot change, people like preachers, counselors, doctors, and teachers are wasting their time. Thank God that we don't have to wear a sign that says, "Broken Arm" – we know that eventually broken arms can be healed. We don't put a sign on our children saying, "Non-reader" when we send them to school for the first time. We know that most "bumps" are temporary and can be fixed.

In the book of Exodus, Moses was confronted with a bush on fire, given a revelation from God, and commissioned to deliver his people Israel from Egyptian bondage. But in Exodus 3:12, Moses put up a sign. *12 And he said, Certainly I will be with thee; and this shall be a token unto thee, that I have sent thee: When thou hast brought forth the people out of Egypt, ye shall serve God upon this mountain.*

But in the next verse God said, "I will be with you."

Again in Exodus 4:10, Moses puts up a sign:

10 And Moses said unto the LORD, O my Lord, I am not eloquent, neither heretofore, nor since thou hast spoken unto thy servant: but I am slow of speech, and of a slow tongue.

The Lord answered in the next several verses:

11 And the LORD said unto him, who hath made man's mouth? or who maketh the dumb, or deaf, or the seeing, or the blind? have not I the LORD?

12 Now therefore go, and I will be with thy mouth, and teach thee what thou shalt say.

13 And he said, O my Lord, send, I pray thee, by the hand of him whom thou wilt send.

14 And the anger of the LORD was kindled against Moses, and he said, Is not Aaron the Levite thy brother? I know that he can speak well. And also, behold, he cometh forth to meet thee: and when he seeth thee, he will be glad in his heart.

Again, and again in the Scriptures we see God repairing various "bumps" in the road. You may think of several, but my favorite is "I can't give birth; I'm a virgin!"

Let us pray,

Our Father,

As we run into our many bumps in our own lives, help us to remember your promise given to us in Exodus 3:12: *"I will be with you."*

In Your name we pray,

Amen

Story 6

"I am the true vine..." (John 15:1)

People who don't know me very well know me as the former principal in Mr. Rogers' neighborhood at West End Elementary School. However, people that know me well know me as "Sandra's yardman" because that is my passion. I am not bragging, but whether we lived in Fitzgerald, LaGrange, or Rome, I have always had the prettiest yard on my street. Well, I guess I am bragging, but I am the one telling this story, so I can brag if I want to.

My pride in my yardwork goes back to my childhood. I was raised by a poor family in South Alabama. When other children in Fort Deposit were getting motorbikes from their parents, my father bought three old lawn mowers for me and my two brothers. Now, if you lived in Fort Deposit and didn't cut your own lawn, it was cut by the Rogers boys. First, I cut with my older brother, then when he got a real job and went to college, I cut with my younger brother. It was nothing for us to play a football game on Friday night and get up early on Saturday morning and cut ten to twelve yards before dark.

I have a very "high maintenance" yard now. Besides picking up sticks and limbs and cutting my grass every week, I have a regular time schedule. The last week in September I aerate, over seed and fertilize my turf fescue. I have a million trees, so from the first of October until the first of January, I blow and rake leaves and haul them away. In November, I do all the major pruning of my many hollies and evergreens. The last week of February, I spend about four afternoons cutting my monkey grass. I pray every summer for regular rain, so I don't have to spend day after day watering my grass, plants and shrubs.

I do all my yardwork myself except for applying chemicals. I am not very good with chemicals. My wife says, "The only thing you kill are your brain cells". One day, my chemical company was spraying my shrubs and plants. I went out to talk to the worker and he reminded me to prune or cut off any dead branches from my many azaleas, camelias, rhododendrons and other plants.

Disciples IV Class – This reminded me of the first eight verses of the 15th chapter of John. Jesus says,

1 I am the true vine, and my Father is the husbandman.

2 Every branch in me that beareth not fruit he taketh away: and every branch that beareth fruit, he purgeth it, that it may bring forth more fruit.

3 Now ye are clean through the word which I have spoken unto you.

4 Abide in me, and I in you. As the branch cannot bear fruit of itself, except it abide in the vine; no more can ye, except ye abide in me.

5 I am the vine, ye are *the branches: He that abideth in me, and I in him, the same bringeth forth much fruit: for without me ye can do nothing.*

6 If a man abide not in me, he is cast forth as a branch, and is withered; and men gather them, and cast them *into the fire, and they are burned.*

7 If ye abide in me, and my words abide in you, ye shall ask what ye will, and it shall be done unto you.

8 Herein is my Father glorified, that ye bear much fruit; so shall ye be my disciples.

In His final farewell to His disciples, Jesus used this vineyard metaphor to challenge his disciples. The vine grower, the vine, and the branches make up the metaphor – the Father who "planted"; Jesus, the vine; and disciples, the branches. A vine exists for one purpose – to bear great clusters of ripe fruit. Disciples are meant to live "in Christ" and to bear the fruit of discipleship.

Some vines show promise of fruit; others do not. Worthless branches are pruned away so the vine's energy can flow into the fruited branches. The whole point – for the vine growers, vine, and branches – is the fruit. What is the fruit? And the fruit is the same for the branches as it was for the vine, the same for disciples as it was for Jesus' earthly ministry – to invite people to hear, believe, and obey the Word. In other words, to witness for Him.

Jesus knew disciples could be drawn to other loyalties. Branches lying on the ground can root themselves, but those roots are shallow. Separated from the central vine, they lose their vitality. They bear little fruit. They usually die.

John 15:5 - *I am the vine, ye are the branches: He that abideth in me, and I in him, the same bringeth forth much fruit: for without me ye can do nothing.*

While I learned very early in life the rewards of gardening and yardwork, I struggle every day to apply the biblical meaning of insuring that the "true vine" remains vital and alive in me. I pray every day that I stay attached to this vine and do not get pruned or cut off. I believe Jesus' plan for us all as branches of the true vine is to help each other bear fruit for Christ by witnessing to others.

Jack Rogers

Story 7

Problem Solvers

During the entire decade of the 1980s in LaGrange, I was in a weekly Bible study group that met every Wednesday night. One of the members of that group was a Registrar at LHS. Now he was a little different from the rest of us in that he traded cars about every five or six months. When we saw him in a new car, we gave him a hard time, as you could imagine. His answer was always the same – "There are two kinds of people – talkers and doers". Of course, he was implying that he was a doer, and we just talked about it.

During that same decade, I was Athletic Director at LHS, and part of my job was to resolve differences between football and basketball coaches as well as all of the different high school sports. Guess what sport required more of my problem-solving abilities than any other sport? You probably guessed it – cheerleading.

When I became a principal, I found myself resolving problems between students; between students and teachers; between teachers and parents; between parents; between teachers and assistant principals; between custodians; between cafeteria personnel and the list goes on and on. I soon found myself classifying people into two distinct groups – different from the Registrar's two groups – those that create problems and those that solve problems. I'm sure that you know people that fall into either of these groups.

Now there are a lot of people that fall into the group of problem-solvers. If you have a toothache, your dentist is your problem-solver; if you have a heart attack, your doctor is your problem-solver; if you have a flat tire, your tire company may be your problem-solver; if you have a spiritual problem, then your preacher may be your problem-solver.

Who is the ultimate problem-solver? My belief is that Jesus is the ultimate problem-solver. We know that he solved a lot of physical problems. In the second chapter of John, John tells us that Jesus turned six jars of water into wine when the host ran out of wine at the wedding feast. In the sixth chapter of John, Jesus fed five-thousand men, in addition to the women and children, from five small barley loaves and two small fish. Jesus healed many – the man with leprosy; the paralytic; the man with demons; the dead girl; the sick woman; the deaf and dumb man; the boy with the evil spirit; the blind man, and many more.

But, in order to be the ultimate problem-solver, you must solve the ultimate problem. My belief is the ultimate problem is how should sinners, such as you and me, be saved?

We are all sinners, each in our own way. Now I'm a pretty good fellow – there are some of the Ten Commandments that I follow. I have never murdered anybody, never have committed adultery or cheated on my wife and I try to worship God on a regular basis. Then there are the buts.... some things God does not approve of. My former superintendent said that I see everything as either black or white – there is no gray area with me. When you see everything as either right or wrong you tend to be more judgmental than most – and I admit that I am very judgmental. But in Luke 6:37, Jesus says, *"Judge not, and ye shall not be judged...."*

The first commandment in Exodus 20:3 tells us, *Thou shalt have no other gods before me.*

But there are times when I put my possessions ahead of Him. Other times I put golf ahead of Him. Sometimes, I put my granddaughters first, my wife first, and I almost always put myself ahead of Him.

If we are all sinners, then how can we be saved? Jesus solved the ultimate problem. He died on the cross for the forgiveness of our sins – yours and mine. Savior is synonymous with the title of the Son of God, Christ the Lord. His mission to save His people from their sins was announced before His birth (Matthew 1:21) and was stated by Jesus as the aim of His coming (Luke 19:10). The salvation that he wrought is for all mankind; He is "the Savior of the world" (John 4:42 and I John 4:14).

Story 8

Traveling Without a Driver

How many times do we go traveling through life without a driver?

I have never been much of a water person, and now that I have such a passion for golf, I never enjoy water sports at all. When we lived near West Point Lake in the early 1980s, I owned a ski boat for two years. At the end of the two years, I could count only seven times that I put the boat in the lake. It was occupying half of my garage for no practical reason, so I sold it.

One of my most memorable experiences did happen on a boating trip in the late 1960s. I graduated from college with a B.A. degree in math with no education courses, so when I started teaching, I had to go to Georgia Southern College in Statesboro for two summers to get certified to teach.

One of our friends at Fitzgerald High School was a business teacher. Before he got married, he spent his summers with his parents. They lived near Cobbtown, which was not too far from Statesboro. For three consecutive weeks, he invited an industrial arts teacher and me down to a large lake near Cobbtown to water ski. Since there were three of us, one of us would ski, and one would drive the boat while the other one rested on the shore. On that third outing I had just finished skiing and was resting on the shore. He was driving his boat and our other friend skiing. I looked up to see the driver sitting on the side of the boat driving full speed down the middle of the lake. All of a sudden, I saw him fall off the side of his boat. The driverless boat was still going full speed with our friend hanging on to the ski rope. After going another hundred yards or so, he wised up and dropped the ski line. The boat hit the embankment going full speed, jumped up about five yards in the air and went at least another twenty-five yards before it landed. Thank the Lord no one was hurt.

Since then I have thought about that afternoon hundreds of times. The memory of that driverless boat going full speed across the lake with the skier still skiing as though nothing had happened is permanently embedded in my memory. Isn't that the same way we live our lives if we don't have God in charge driving our boat? We are going through life, traveling at speeds up to fifty miles an hour and headed straight toward an embankment and disaster of one kind or other.

All of us need Jesus to be our driver. Unfortunately, all of us do not accept Him. When Jesus called his disciples by saying, "Come, follow me," He was making an absolute demand. For Jesus to be the driver of their boat meant leaving something, someone or some place behind. To obey meant to walk into the unknown unencumbered – ready to listen, to learn, to witness, to serve. The word disciple means "learner".

Simon and Andrew, James and John left their fishing nets and relatives. Matthew, also called Levi, left his tax office.

Jesus offered other persons radical discipleship, or to drive their boat, but they would not break loose from the things that held them. Jesus warned a scribe, a prospective disciple, that He would often be sleeping on the ground. Matthew 8:19-20 tells us that we hear no more from the man.

Another man wanted to wait until his elderly father died. Matthew 8:21-22

21 And another of his disciples said unto him, Lord, suffer me first to go and bury my father.

22 But Jesus said unto him, Follow me; and let the dead bury their dead.

Still later, a rich man considered discipleship. Matthew 19:16-22

16 And, behold, one came and said unto him, Good Master, what good thing shall I do, that I may have eternal life?

17 And he said unto him, Why callest thou me good? There is none good but one, that is, God: but if thou wilt enter into life, keep the commandments.

18 He saith unto him, Which? Jesus said, Thou shalt do no murder, Thou shalt not commit adultery, Thou shalt not steal, Thou shalt not bear false witness,

19 Honour thy father and thy mother: and, Thou shalt love thy neighbour as thyself.

20 The young man saith unto him, All these things have I kept from my youth up: what lack I yet?

21 Jesus said unto him, If thou wilt be perfect, go and sell that thou hast, and give to the poor, and thou shalt have treasure in heaven: and come and follow me.

22 But when the young man heard that saying, he went away sorrowful: for he had great possessions.

Jesus offers all of us the same choice; let Him be the driver of our boat or we will hang relentlessly on to the ski rope with someone or something else driving. The choice is ours.

Let us pray,

Our Father help us to follow your command to "Come, follow me".

In Your name we pray,

Amen

Story 9

Why have I been targeted?

Late one Friday afternoon, I was turning into my driveway in my truck when a teenage driver hit the back-passenger side panel of my truck. It felt like I had been side-swiped riding one of those bumper cars at the fair.

I didn't think too much about it until about two months later when I was leaving a Friday night football game at our stadium. I stopped at the red light where 2nd Avenue feeds into Shorter Avenue. The light turned green, and the lady in the first car started through the light. She must have panicked when she saw cars coming down Shorter Avenue toward the red light. She slammed on her brakes. The man in the SUV behind her slammed on his brakes and missed her. I slammed on my brakes behind him and missed him. Unfortunately, the man coming up quickly behind me saw a green light and kept on going – right into the back of my car – forcing my car into the back of the SUV. I had damage on both ends of my car. After being hit from behind twice in an eight-week period, I began to wonder if I had a target painted on the back of my vehicles.

However, my feelings of being targeted were small compared to Job's feelings in the Old Testament. In Job 7:20, Job asked, *I have sinned; what shall I do unto thee, O thou preserver of men? why hast thou set me as a mark against thee, so that I am a burden to myself?*

Job 1:1 - *There was a man in the land of Uz, whose name was Job; and that man was perfect and upright, and one that feared God, and eschewed evil.*

Job was a wealthy man in many ways but suffered tragedies in bunches – first he lost his animals and servants, then his family. All were gone. Job tore his robe in mourning, shaved his head, but was able to say, *Naked came I out of my mother's womb, and naked shall I return thither: the LORD gave, and the LORD hath taken away; blessed be the name of the LORD.* Job 1:21

Then came a second test – sores from the bottom of his feet to the top of his head. Job went into shock. He sat among the ashes for seven days and seven nights.

Calamity had come to him. The fundamental beliefs upon which Job built his life – faithfulness and obedience to God, practice of righteous ways that brought him health, happiness, family, and prosperity - had been called in to question.

Job wonders why he has been targeted. Job and his three friends were trapped in the idea that sin caused suffering. Job must have sinned, or his children must have sinned, and Job is suffering because of their sins. They reasoned that if God is just and righteous, someone must be to blame.

Job wanted to make his case before God, but God spoke out of the whirlwind. God challenges Job's desire to understand the whys of good and evil, suffering and happiness, life and death. God says that Job's friends were wrong about their neat reward-and punishment rules.

God answered Job, not by removing the mysteries, but by being present for Job. Job's painful prayer had been answered: God came to him.

Job understood that chaos is part of God's creation. Life is beyond our control. So is God. Coming into the presence of God was all that mattered to Job. He was content to live with mystery. And to trust the God who created him.

Our Father,

Thank You for assuring us of Your presence, even when we experience suffering and injustice and ask questions that are not answered.

Amen

Story 10

Forgiveness

Sometimes it is hard to forgive others; other times it is even harder to ask for forgiveness. You may get tired of my coaching stories, but I am going to tell you two more: one in which I forgave and one in which I had to ask for forgiveness.

While I was coaching at Fitzgerald High School in the late 1960s, my wife began getting very obscene telephone calls at night while I was coaching. Of course, the calls scared her to death since I was gone so much of the time coaching football, basketball and baseball.

We contacted the police, and after the third call they put a call tracer on our phone. After a few weeks, our principal called Sandra and me to his office to meet with a detective.

To our total shock and surprise, we found that the obscene caller was none other than my very quiet and shy little second baseman on my baseball team. We knew his parents well. They were a farming family and very strict Church of Christ believers. They were at church every time it opened and did not let their son attend any fun school events, such as dances and parties. He was a high school junior who had bottled up a lot of emotions, typical of teenage boys, which he expressed in obscene telephone calls to Sandra and a mother of another baseball player, my shortstop. He was really a good kid who had never said anything to me but "Yes sir" and "No sir." After talking with the police and his parents, we agreed not to press charges if he and his parents received professional counseling. I later called him to the office and told him that I had forgiven him, and he could continue to play baseball, which he did his junior and senior years.

We had a very good football program at Fitzgerald. In fact, we only lost five regular season games in five years. I was also the head basketball coach and during the football playoffs each year I would practice football after school and then at night. I would have basketball tryouts and practice for the non-football players after school. My second year as head coach we had about three weeks of night practices before the football playoffs ended. When the playoffs ended, we only had one practice on Monday before we played our first game on Tuesday night against Moultrie High School. In a small AA school like that all your best athletes play all the sports, and my best five basketball players, by far, were all football players. My plan, as a young coach who didn't' know better, was to start the five football players and to substitute the non-football players as the game went on. But the game was one of those in which neither team led by more than two or three points the whole game. I got so involved in winning the game that I didn't make a single substitution the whole game. The next night a little junior guard that had practiced for three weeks and not gotten into the game called me in tears and said that I had destroyed his confidence.

Of course, he was right and in a roundabout way I apologized to him. In my heart I knew that he was right and my desire to win had kept me from doing the right thing. It was a lesson I remembered as long as I coached. I needed to be forgiven.

In Luke 17:4, Christ taught that forgiveness is a duty and that no limit should be set to the extent of forgiveness. Matthew 18:34-35 and Luke 15:28-30 tells us that an unforgiving spirit is one of the most serious of sins. God forgives our sins because of the atoning death of Jesus.

In Matthew 18:21-22, *Then came Peter to him, and said, Lord, how oft shall my brother sin against me, and I forgive him? till seven times? 22 Jesus saith unto him, I say not unto thee, Until seven times: but, Until seventy times seven.*

Then Jesus tells the parable of the Unmerciful Servant. A king wanted to settle accounts with his servants. A man who owed him ten thousand talents was brought to him. The master ordered that he and his wife and children and all that he had be sold to repay the debt.

The servant fell on his knees and begged. The servant's master took pity on him, cancelled the debt and let him go.

But when the servant went out, he found one of his fellow servants who owed him a hundred denarii. He grabbed him and began to choke him.

His fellow servant fell to his knees and begged him, but he refused. Instead, he went off and had the man thrown into prison until he could pay the debt. When the other servants saw what had happened, they were greatly distressed and went and told their master everything that had happened.

Then the master called the servant in. In anger the master turned him over to the jailers until he should pay back all he owed.

Matthew tells us in 18:35, *So likewise shall my heavenly Father do also unto you, if ye from your hearts forgive not everyone his brother their trespasses.*

Let us pray,

Our Father,

Help us not to be like the unmerciful servant but to be willing to forgive seventy-seven times as commanded by your son Jesus.

In Your name we pray,

Amen.

Story 11

Doing the Right Thing

Doing the right thing! Why is it so hard? We see examples of people not doing the right thing every day. The military guards at the prison in Iraq abused their prisoners. Even though it represented only twelve or fifteen soldiers out of the nearly two-hundred thousand soldiers in Iraq, it sure has reflected badly on our military and our country as a whole.

The CEO's and CFO's at several large corporations made hundreds of millions of dollars while leaving their employees, investors and stockholders without jobs and without retirement. They didn't do the right thing.

Every election year the campaign ads become more negative and more vicious. Is it because politicians can't do the right thing? Even closer to home, are we as voters not doing the right thing by voting for the candidate that uses the most negative ads?

Why don't we do the right thing? The answer is simple. We do not follow the second commandment as given to us in Exodus 20:4,

Thou shalt not make unto thee any graven image, or any likeness of anything that is in heaven above, or that is in the earth beneath, or that is in the water under the earth: We don't do the right thing because we

consciously or unconsciously worship idols such as money, power, pleasure or the pursuit of these things.

We don't do the right thing! However, it is not because we don't have examples of the right thing to do or role models who did the right thing.

Take the book of Daniel in the Old Testament, Daniel and his friends, Shadrach, Meshach and Abednego found themselves uprooted from home and family in a strange kind of exile by the Babylonians' siege of Jerusalem. Young, foreign-born and captive, yet because of their noble birth, their wisdom and intelligence, they were selected to be trained for royal service.

The King assigned them a daily portion of the royal - rations of food and wine. To the oppressed, food rich extravagant food is always a symbol of power. However, Daniel and his companions chose not to "defile" themselves by eating rich food, but rather chose to eat fruits and vegetables and drink water instead.

Daniel's three friends, Shadrach, Meshach, and Abednego were caught refusing to bow down before Nebuchadnezzar's golden statue. For the young men the commandments were clear: Exodus 20:4, *Thou shalt not make unto thee any graven image, or any likeness of anything that* is *in heaven above, or that* is *in the earth beneath, or that* is *in the water under the earth:*

The young men replied to the king in Daniel 3:17-18:

17 If it be so, our God whom we serve is able to deliver us from the burning fiery furnace, and he will deliver us out of thine hand, O king.

18 But if not, be it known unto thee, O king, that we will not serve thy gods, nor worship the golden image which thou hast set up. What courage these young men showed in the face of fire.

Daniel, like devout Jews across the centuries, prayed three times a day – in the morning, in the afternoon, and at night. King Darius decreed that anyone who prayed to any god or man, except to the king himself, would be thrown into the lions' den. Daniel continued to pray to God and was thrown into the lions' den. God shut the mouths of the lions and Daniel was not injured.

Daniel and his companion did the right thing. They did not fall into the trap of worshiping false gods. We have good role models. THE QUESTION IS: Can we BE good role models as well?

Let us pray,

Our Father,

Help us to follow the example of Daniel and his companions by doing the right thing in everything we do.

Amen.

Story 12

Excellent Sprinters – Good Marathons

I never intended to run a marathon. After all, 26.2 miles is a long way. And besides that, I was fifty-six years old, weighed over two-hundred pounds, and was built more like a tight end in football than a marathon runner. However, the new principal at our high school and I had become good friends and running buddies. We had run in several of the 5K and 10K races around Rome as well as running to relieve tension and stress from work. I called it "sweating the poison out".

One night at a basketball game we began talking about running and challenged each other to run a marathon. We decided on one in Charlotte, N.C. because it was during our spring break. We started training at Berry College and taking our long runs on Saturday morning.

We were already running six miles, so every two or three weeks we worked in increments of 8, 10, 12, 14, 16, 18 and finally, 22 miles one Saturday including running the snow trail up to the house of dreams.

Finally, April 10, 1999 arrived, and we met in Charlotte. We had not properly researched and didn't realize that this was one of the most difficult marathons in the U.S. The last eight or ten miles were up and down hills that were a long as four tenth of a mile. After about sixteen or seventeen miles I ran into the "wall" that everyone talks about, and even with his best encouragement I had to walk more than run the last nine or ten miles.

I loved running, and it became a passion for me. I ran two more marathons in the next two years, even though I had to walk a good part of each one of them. At over two-hundred pounds, I ran in the "Clydesdale" division. The only things I passed were parked cars. In fact, I was training for a fourth marathon when I hurt my back. Now I can't even run to the end of my driveway.

Our Bible mentions running and racing many times.

I Corinthians 9:24 *Know ye not that they which run in a race run all, but one receiveth the prize? So run, that ye may obtain.*

2 Timothy 4:7 *I have fought a good fight, I have finished my course, I have kept the faith:*

Hebrews 12:1 *Wherefore seeing we also are compassed about with so great a cloud of witnesses, let us lay aside every weight, and the sin which doth so easily beset us, and let us run with patience the race that is set before us,*

Revelation 14:12 *Here is the patience of the saints: here are they that keep the commandments of God, and the faith of Jesus.*

We just completed a very effective five-year strategic plan for our church. Our leader gave us great insight and direction. I agreed with 99% of his comments and advice. There was one thing I questioned. He said that our society had become an "excellent sprinter" one and not one of a good marathoner, and in order to attract new people into our church we must become an "excellent sprinter" church. By this he meant more one-time programs and not long-term ones. He gave the example of a youth choir giving a concert with only one or two practices.

I agree that this will help attract more new people into our congregation, but I question if we can keep them for the long-term if we only have a "quick or excellent sprinter" mentality.

We are very fortunate in our church to have many marathon activities. The men's prayer breakfast has been meeting for how many years? Sandra and I were in the same Sunday School class since we moved to Rome in 1989. Some of you have met in the same Sunday School class for thirty to forty years. Sandra and I took three thirty-four-week Disciple classes. Some of you have sung in the choir for thirty or forty years. We are very fortunate to have many marathon programs in our church.

Let us pray,

Our Father,

Help us to be marathon runners in our faith and service to you and your kingdom here on earth.

Amen

Story 13

"I am the Bread of Life"

One of my jobs while working my way through college was serving as assistant dormitory director my senior year. It was not a bad job. It paid my board and meals. The downside was that I had to stay on duty every other weekend from 6:00 p.m. Friday until 6:00 p.m. on Sunday, except for meals.

During those long weekends, I became friends with our dormitory director. He had gone through college with my older brother. I noticed that he ate only one meal a day. I asked him about it, and he said that he had lost one-hundred and sixty pounds. I was impressed. I asked him what his motivation was. He said that about two years ago he woke up one morning and saw a huge banner across the front of our dormitory reading, "HOME OF THE GREAT WHITE WHALE". What a motivation to lose weight.

My wife and I have probably lost over five-hundred pounds since we got married thirty-eight years ago. We would lose ten pounds one month and gain eleven pounds the following month. We lost fifteen and gained thirteen back. How many of you have played this game?

In one of my graduate courses we were studying "comfort levels". The teacher was making the point that we can never accomplish anything of any importance unless we are willing to rise out of our comfort level. He asked each of us to define our comfort level. I said mine was sitting at our breakfast room table eating a large plate of country fried steak over white rice and brown gravy. On the side would be a basket of crescent rolls and of course, since I am from South Alabama, a little ketchup on the side of the plate.

Jesus tells us that we are too concerned about physical food and not concerned enough about spiritual food.

John 6:35 says, *And Jesus said unto them, I am the bread of life: he that cometh to me shall never hunger; and he that believeth on me shall never thirst.*

We see examples in the Old and New Testament of God feeding his people. God, through Moses, mandated the Feast of Unleavened Bread (Passover) so that Israel would remember those four-hundred years of slavery in Egypt.

The festival also recalled those forty wearisome years when their ancestors wandered in the wilderness stomachs cramped with hunger, throats parched with thirst. The Israelites would have died in that barren desert if God had not provided manna, which means literally, "What is it?".

Exodus 16:15 *And when the children of Israel saw it, they said one to another, It is manna: for they wist not what it was. And Moses said unto them, This is the bread which the LORD hath given you to eat.*

Exodus 16:31 *And the house of Israel called the name thereof Manna: and it was like coriander seed, white; and the taste of it was like wafers made with honey.*

Exodus 16: 19-20
19 And Moses said, Let no man leave of it till the morning.

20 Notwithstanding they hearkened not unto Moses; but some of them left of it until the morning, and it bred worms, and stank: and Moses was wroth with them. Manna could not be saved up, except for manna gathered on the sixth day for Sabbath food.

Manna is the force behind Matthew 6:11 *Give us this day our daily bread.*

Jesus' feeding of the five thousand in the New Testament is easily compared to manna in the wilderness:

1. Jesus and the disciples crossed the Sea of Galilee. Moses and the Israelites also crossed the sea.

2. Everyone was tired, hungry, and far from any village. Just as with Moses in the wilderness, thousands of people needed food.

3. The resources were meager – five tiny barley loaves and two salted, dried sardine-like fish. Barley was considered the grain of the poor. The situation seemed hopeless, just as in Exodus.

4. Everyone had enough manna. Jesus had food left over, enough to fill twelve baskets. God is extravagant!

After feeding the five thousand, Jesus proclamation, "I am the bread of life," moved the discussion from physical bread that God provides to the spiritual "bread" that gives abundant and eternal life.

When Jesus said in the synagogue,

John 6:53 *Then Jesus said unto them, Verily, verily, I say unto you, Except ye eat the flesh of the Son of man, and drink his blood, ye have no life in you.*

Many followers complained because Jews were forbidden to eat blood. The crowds scattered, leaving only the faithful twelve.

The crowd could not comprehend the deeper meanings. To "eat" and "drink" meant to trust Jesus, to follow Him, obey Him, to feed on His spirit and to believe in Him as the nourisher of life.

Wouldn't our lives improve if we were to resolve to increase our intake of the spiritual bread of life instead of our annual resolution to cut back on intake of physical nourishment?

Let us pray,

Our Father,

Thank You for being the "bread of life" and providing our spiritual needs. Help us to concern ourselves more with the spiritual and less with our physical needs in every activity we undertake this week.

In Your name we pray,

Amen.

Story 14

There is a real Santa Claus

Like most small children I believed in Santa Claus, but I was in my late twenties before I knew that there was a real Santa Claus. My oldest son was five or six years old and in his "letter to Santa" he requested a car racing set. I was coaching basketball at the time, and we were in a pre-Christmas tournament that took most of my time. I did purchase the racing set and a 4x6 piece of ¾ inch plywood on which to mount it, but like most young and foolish men, I waited until Christmas Eve to put it together. Besides, I didn't have a place to hide it in the small house we were renting at the time. Finally, about 11:00 p.m. when Jeff was sound asleep, I took out the plywood from the attic and the racing set to start assembling it. The directions seemed so simple. By around 1:00 or 1:30 p.m. I had it fully assembled and ready for a test run. Nothing happened!!! It wouldn't move! Not even one inch!

Beginning to get frustrated, I took it apart and started all over again. Again, nothing happened!!! It would not run!!

Getting more frustrated and exhausted, I took up each section of the track and replaced it --- one section at a time---. Again, nothing worked!!! It would not run!!!

Finally, around 4:00 a.m., I decided I would just tell Jeff that Santa Claus had given him the set and it was our job to get it running. At 4 a.m. that sounded like the perfect solution, so I went to bed.

Two hours later at around 6:00 a.m., I awoke to hear something going around and around. ZOOM!!! ZOOM!!! ZOOM!!!

I got up in an exhausted daze and went in the living room to see Jeff racing the cars around and around the track. I thought, "Sometime in the last two hours Santa Claus came into our house and fixed what I had not been able to fix the night before in order for the prized racing set to work perfectly. There is a Santa Claus!!! For real, there is a Santa Claus." (Of course, the problem might have been that I was trying to run the cars clockwise and Jeff had them running counterclockwise). Nevertheless, there is a real Santa Claus. That's my story and I'm sticking to it.

In the same sense how do we know there is a real God? I have never seen Him. He has never spoken directly to me – that I know of. How do I know He is real? Yet, I believe strongly in Him. We read the history of His actions and beliefs in the Bible. We read that He sent His son to live among us and teach us how we should live. But this happened two-thousand years ago. How do we know there is a God?

Well, our faith in God has passed the test of time. People have professed their beliefs for hundreds and thousands of years. Our faith is passed on from generation to generation.

When we have reached the end of our rope; when we are totally frustrated and demoralized; who do we turn to? We know that God hears and answers our prayers. We have faith.

Faith is defined as belief and trust in God; knowing that God is real, even though we can't see Him.

Hebrews 11:1 & 6, sums it up completely:

1 *Now faith is the substance of things hoped for, the evidence of things not seen.*

6 *"But without faith* it is *impossible to please* him*: for he that cometh to God must believe that he is, and* that *he is a rewarder of them that diligently seek him."*

Let us pray,

Help us to have faith – to believe and trust in You, and to show our faith by our service for You. In Your name we pray.

Amen.

John 20:29 *Jesus saith unto him, Thomas, because thou hast seen me, thou hast believed: bless-ed are they that have not seen, and yet have be-lieved.*

48

Story 15

Full Moon – Expectations

There is nobody more aware of the timing of a full moon than I am. For all my years as an Assistant Principal, I was the one in the building who handled discipline. I never had to look outside at night to know when a full moon was approaching. I always had more fights, more confrontations, and more bad things happen in the days leading up to a full moon. After the full moon passed, things always settled back to normal. I used to work very closely with the local police and their statistics and records showed a twenty percent increase in crime in days leading up to a full moon. They often prepared for this by having extra staff during these days. I also communicated with hospital personnel who said emergency room activity increased by twenty to forty percent during the days leading up to a full moon.

I have often wondered how much of this full-moon activity is affected by our expectations of negative things happening and how much is reality. You see, I am a strong believer that our expectations of future events strongly affect the outcome of these events. Generally, if we expect good things to happen, they will; and conversely, if we expect bad things to happen, they usually do. I find this especially true of athletics. This is one reason I admire the way Tiger Woods plays golf. He expects to win every time he plays, and he wins more than his share.

I went to the University of Alabama when Bear Bryant was coaching. He expected to win every game he played, even though most of his athletes were recruited from the state of Alabama. He won about fifteen SEC championships as well as several national titles.

I found expectations play a large role in education. My basic philosophy is that children, no matter what age, will generally do what is expected of them if you communicate those expectations on a regular and consistent basis.

Expectation plays a large part in religion also. In two different verses the book of Proverbs expresses the expectations of the wicked.

In Proverbs 10:28 *The hope of the righteous shall be gladness: but the expectation of the wicked shall perish.*

Proverbs 11:23 says, *The desire of the righteous is only good: but the expectation of the wicked is wrath.*

The book of Psalms tells us that our expectations should come from God.
Psalms 62:5-8 says:

5 My soul, wait thou only upon God; for my expectation is from him.

6 He only is my rock and my salvation: he is my defence; I shall not be moved.

7 In God is my salvation and my glory: the rock of my strength, and my refuge, is in God.

8 Trust in him at all times; ye people, pour out your heart before him: God is a refuge for us. Selah.

In the New Testament, Paul expressed his expectation of service in his letter to the Philippians.

In Philippians 1:20-21 Paul says, *20 According to my earnest expectation and my hope, that in nothing I shall be ashamed, but that with all boldness, as always, so now also Christ shall be magnified in my body, whether it be by life, or by death.*

21 For to me to live is Christ, and to die is gain.

The recent events in the life of our church fall like a full moon on us all. We each need to be aware of our expectations for where this church will go from here. In the last six months of 2004, almost everyone went to our church council meetings expecting confrontation, argument and disagreement. And we were not disappointed. In the first council meeting of 2005, I was very heartened to hear a church leader speak at length about the anticipation of a great year in the life of our church. Another church leader followed that up with positive expectations of our finances for 2005.

We also have a great opportunity to exercise our positive expectations in welcoming our new pastor in July. If we expect the Bishop to stick it to us because of our treatment of our last minister, then that is what we will get. However, if we expect exactly the right person to pastor our church next year, we will get that person.

Let us pray,

Our Father,
Help us not to expect a full moon, but to expect our church to faithfully minister not only to our own members, but to extend our ministry to all people in need in our community.

In Your name we pray,

Amen.

Story 16

Security

I have never even dreamed about getting old enough to draw Social Security, but I recently went down to their local office to fill out an application. That got me to thinking. What is security? Many people think that if you have lots of money, then you are secure. However, if your money is in stock, all it would take is two or three major terrorist attack weapons of mass destruction and stock wouldn't be worth the paper it is written on. If our money is in CDs, we all know that banks can go under just like they did during the depression in the 1930s. We can own real estate, but a major tornado or hurricane can completely destroy that. Now that I've got you thoroughly depressed, then I ask the question again, "What is security?".

Our dictionary defines security as:

 a) freedom from dangers; safety b) freedom from fear or anxiety c) freedom from want or deprivation

Where and how do we get security? Years ago, like many of you, I had a security system, put in my house. Now that is a whole new story. I remember the first time we put a security system in our school. Every time the alarm went off, even in the middle of the night, I had to meet the police at the front door, and we had to walk through every room to guarantee it was secure, even if it was in the middle of the night.

I remember the telephone rang about 2:00 a.m. in the morning on one of the coldest nights of the winter. It took me about fifteen minutes to get to the school. The alarm code said that the problem was in the waiting room of the office. The afternoon before, our Assistant Principal (bless her soul) had taped valentines all around the top of the room with the name and birthdays of every teacher in the building. There in the middle of the room was the art teacher's valentine on the floor. It had fluttered down from the top of the room in the middle of the night, setting off the motion detector. Now you know why I retired at such a relatively young age.

Where do we find security? Where do we find freedom from danger; freedom from want or fear; freedom from pain or suffering?

The book of Psalms has answers to all our questions:

Psalm 9:9-10; Psalm 46:1-2; Psalm 62:1-8; Psalm 91:2-4; Psalm 142:5-7

Where do we go for security? God is our refuge and strength. He alone is the true source of security.

Let us pray,

Help us not to trust man for our inner strength and security. Help us to trust You alone.

In Your name we pray,

Amen.

Story 17

God Judges All People

I remember when Sandra and I moved to Georgia from Alabama in August of 1967. I was the Junior Varsity football and Junior Varsity basketball coach and Algebra II teacher at Fitzgerald High School in South Georgia. The head football coach was a legend in those parts. He was the last coach in Georgia to run the Notre Dame box. He was a rugged-looking man with a bald head. That is, he shaved what little hair he had on the sides of his head. He owned a farm about five miles out of town. He used to go by the high school cafeteria after practice to pick up the scraps from lunch to feed his pigs. He was a tough man and a tough coach. He told his players that he was never going to go on the field during a game after an injured player unless that player needed an ambulance to carry him off. As a result, his players were as tough as he was. I remember one Friday night during a game, a small senior linebacker, ran off the field with a crushed kneecap rather than have Coach come out on the field for him.

Coach was a tough man, and I remember how shocked I was when he invited Sandra and me to dinner one weekend on his farm. It didn't take me long to realize that as tough as he was, his wife was the boss of that household. His three girls also had him wrapped around their fingers. Guess what! Coach was not as tough as I thought he was.

As a principal, I was known as the "suspending" principal. If students couldn't behave, I just sent them home. My superintendent once said, "You see everything in black and white". He said, "There is no gray area with you" and he was right! I tend to judge people as good or bad, positive or negative. I don't spend any time with people that I don't like or people with negative attitudes. A long time ago I decided life was too short to spend any time with people that I don't like or people with a negative attitude.

Having this tendency to judge others, I was the perfect person to have to teach the Sunday School lesson on the second Sunday in March. The title of the Lesson was, "God Judges All People" and the scripture for the lesson was Romans 2:1-16 which reads as follows:

1 Therefore thou art inexcusable, O man, whosoever thou art that judgest: for wherein thou judgest another, thou condemnest thyself; for thou that judgest doest the same things.

2 But we are sure that the judgment of God is according to truth against them which commit such things.

3 And thinkest thou this, O man, that judgest them which do such things, and doest the same, that thou shalt escape the judgment of God?

4 Or despisest thou the riches of his goodness and forbearance and longsuffering; not knowing that the goodness of God leadeth thee to repentance?

5 But after thy hardness and impenitent heart treas-urest up unto thyself wrath against the day of wrath and revelation of the righteous judgment of God;

6 Who will render to every man according to his deeds:

7 To them who by patient continuance in well doing seek for glory and honour and immortality, eternal life:

8 But unto them that are contentious, and do not obey the truth, but obey unrighteousness, indignation and wrath,

9 Tribulation and anguish, upon every soul of man that doeth evil, of the Jew first, and also of the Gentile;

10 But glory, honour, and peace, to every man that worketh good, to the Jew first, and also to the Gentile:

11 For there is no respect of persons with God.

12 For as many as have sinned without law shall also perish without law: and as many as have sinned in the law shall be judged by the law;

13 For not the hearers of the law are just before God, but the doers of the law shall be justified.

14 For when the Gentiles, which have not the law, do by nature the things contained in the law, these, hav-ing not the law, are a law unto themselves:

15 Which shew the work of the law written in their hearts, their conscience also bearing witness, and their thoughts the mean while accusing or else excusing one another;)

16 In the day when God shall judge the secrets of men by Jesus Christ according to my gospel.

Several aspects of Paul's letter to the Romans merit special comment. First, God sees our character and conduct for what they are and allows the consequences of our actions to become their own reward or punishment. Secondly, in these same verses, we are reminded that often the things in others we are most prone to criticize are also flaws in our own character and conduct. Thirdly, we are taking advantage of God's mercy by mistakenly presuming that we deserve it. We take for granted that we have earned God's kindness, forbearance, and patience. In reality, these are blessings God gives us. "We" do not deserve these gifts any more than "they" do. All of us are in the same boat: needing grace, receiving grace and called to share grace with one another.

Let us pray,

Help us not to judge others, but to patiently do good and seek your glory and honor.

In your name we pray,

Amen.

Story 18

Cherokee Thought for the Day

One evening, an old Cherokee Indian told his grandson about a "battle" that goes on inside people. He said, "My son, the battle is between two "wolves" inside us all. One is Evil. It is anger, envy, sorrow, regret, guilt, resentment, inferiority, lies, false pride, superiority and ego. The other is Good. It is joy, peace, love, hope, serenity, humility, kindness, benevolence, empathy, generosity, truth, compassion and faith."

The grandson thought about it for a minute and then asked his grandfather, "Which wolf wins?" The old Cherokee simply replied, "The one you feed".

When I read this email, I thought to myself – this is exactly what has been going on in the church for the past year. We have been fighting the battle of two "wolves" inside us. And for many of us we have been feeding the wrong one – the Evil one – anger, greed, resentment, lies, false pride, superiority, ego.

I am a strong believer in positive expectations and that we usually get what we expect to get. The old Cherokee Indian put it another way – we get what we feed.

We may feed "the Evil one," but the Bible tells us what we should be feeding.

Job 6:24 *Teach me, and I will hold my tongue: and cause me to understand wherein I have erred.*

Proverbs 4: 23-27,

23 Keep thy heart with all diligence; for out of it are the issues of life.

24 Put away from thee a froward mouth, and perverse lips put far from thee.

25 Let thine eyes look right on, and let thine eyelids look straight before thee.

26 Ponder the path of thy feet, and let all thy ways be established.

27 Turn not to the right hand nor to the left: remove thy foot from evil.

Proverbs: 6:16-19

16 These six things doth the LORD hate: yea, seven are an abomination unto him:

17 A proud look, a lying tongue, and hands that shed innocent blood,

18 An heart that deviseth wicked imaginations, feet that be swift in running to mischief,

19 A false witness that speaketh lies, and he that soweth discord among brethren.

Proverbs 15:4 *A wholesome tongue is a tree of life: but perverseness therein is a breach in the spirit.*

Proverbs 16:28 *A froward man soweth strife: and a whisperer separateth chief friends.*

Matthew 5:1-12 The Beatitudes:

1 And seeing the multitudes, he went up into a mountain: and when he was set, his disciples came unto him:

2 And he opened his mouth, and taught them, saying,

3 Blessed are the poor in spirit: for theirs is the kingdom of heaven.

4 Blessed are they that mourn: for they shall be comforted.

5 Blessed are the meek: for they shall inherit the earth.

6 Blessed are they which do hunger and thirst after righteousness: for they shall be filled.

7 Blessed are the merciful: for they shall obtain mercy.

8 Blessed are the pure in heart: for they shall see God.

9 Blessed are the peacemakers: for they shall be called the children of God.

10 Blessed are they which are persecuted for righteousness' sake: for theirs is the kingdom of heaven.

11 Blessed are ye, when men shall revile you, and persecute you, and shall say all manner of evil against you falsely, for my sake.

12 Rejoice, and be exceeding glad: for great is your reward in heaven: for so persecuted they the prophets which were before you.

Let us pray,

Help us to follow Your word in feeding the "good" wolf with love, hope, kindness, truth, compassion, and faith.

Amen

Story 19

Things we don't like to do!

We all have things that we don't like to do. Every survey in the last fifty years tells us that people's number one fear is public speaking. Until I was about forty years old, I was very uncomfortable speaking publicly. I have had essential tremors since I was in junior high school and my shaking was very embarrassing to me. Finally, I said forget about it and started having some fun.

Another thing I don't like to do is ask for money. I remember in the very early 1970s my wife and I were participating in the fall financial campaign at the Methodist Church in Fitzgerald, Georgia. That year we used the Circuit Rider method. Our second stop was at a mobile home park. We knocked on the door of the mobile home twice before a very young man answered without shoes or a shirt. Startled, we asked if we could speak to his mother. He hesitated a minute and answered, "She doesn't live here, but my wife does. Would you like to speak to her?" Needless to say, my wife and I excused ourselves.

About three stops later, we found ourselves at the home of a nice older lady. At the time, I was teaching math and coaching football, basketball and baseball. The lady asked us what we did for a living, and I told her that my wife was an English teacher and I taught math, mostly Algebra II. She said, "My daughter's teacher was a coach, and you know coaches make terrible teachers".

Another thing that people don't like is to be disliked by others. About halfway through my professional career I got tired of those long bus trips and getting home at 12:00 and 1:00 o'clock in the morning. I decided to go into administration.

The last fifteen or so years I was the disciplinarian of the school. If you don't want to be liked by a large segment of the school population, be the person who administers discipline. I remember one morning I was in my office with the door closed, drinking my soft drink eating hot cookies from the cafeteria and listening to the radio, preparing to take my morning nap, (Ha-Ha-Ha) when an 8th grader knocked on the door and handed me a taped-closed note from an 8th grade teacher. The note read, "One of my students says John Doe has a gun". I went down to the room and invited the young man to my office. He wore a long, dark trench coat. I asked him to take it off. He did, and under his arm was a shoulder holster with a 357 magnum pistol. Without thinking, I asked him to hand it to me. Luckily, he did.

This reminds me of the story of the mother and her son. She woke him up three times in the morning before he finally asked, "Why do I have to go to school?" She replied, "Because you are forty years old and you are the principal".

The Bible is full of reluctant people who did things that they didn't want to do.

Moses did not want to lead his people from bondage in Egypt. Only after Moses was provided two miraculous signs – Moses' staff was changed to a serpent and his hand became leprous and later was healed – and Moses was assured of Aaron's support in his divine commission to deliver the Israelites from the powerful clutch of Pharaoh, did he succumb to God's will.

Jonah was called to preach at Nineveh because of its great wickedness. Instead of obeying, he took a ship in the opposite direction to Tarshish, probably in SW Spain. His disobedience undoubtedly arose from his fear that the Ninevites would heed his message and repent and that God would forgive the city that had, for many years, grievously oppressed his own land. He was unwilling to be a foreign missionary to a people when he could feel nothing but bitterness. Only after being swallowed by a great fish did Jonah obey and deliver his message.

In the New testament, Paul, then named Saul, was an acknowledged leader in Judaism. His active opposition to Christianity marked him as the natural leader of their persecution. On the road to Damascus the transforming crisis in his life occurred. The three days of fasting in blindness were days of agonizing heart-searching and further dealing with the Lord. Paul's letters refer to it as the work of divine grace and power, transforming him and commissioning him as Christ's messenger.

We all have things we don't want to do, but may be called to do. We hope that we don't have to have our hand become leprous, be swallowed by a whale, or be struck blind for three days to become obedient to His word.

Story 20

"His Time has not yet Come"

Jesus said unto her, I am the resurrection, and the life: he that believeth in me, though he were dead, yet shall he live: John 11:25

Many times in the early part of the book of John, Jesus says, "My time has not yet come". We never know when our time will come.

I was on the coaching staff of the Fitzgerald Purple Hurricanes in 1968. We had a home football game that Friday night. Following the game our 9th grade manager, and his family ate a fish dinner. He got a fishbone stuck in his throat. His parents called the doctor. The doctor told them that he would surgically remove it the next morning. You have all heard that one in a million people are allergic to anesthesia. Well, he was that one. The doctor fought as hard as he could to save him for four long hours. Because of the fishbone accident and the unfortunate allergy to the anesthesia, his time had come far too early in his life.

Until about a year ago, I had never seen a person take his last breath. One afternoon, Sandra and I visited my uncle, in a hospice in Atlanta. As soon as we walked in his room, we knew something was terribly wrong. His wife, children and their spouses were all in tears. His daughter took us outside to tell us that they had been told my uncle would die within the hour. Without a word being said, we sat in the room for nearly an hour before our uncle gasped for breath a couple of times and then passed on to a better place. Because of a series of strokes, our uncle's time had come.

The book of John tells us the story of Jesus raising Lazarus form the dead. When Lazarus became seriously ill, his sisters Mary and Martha believed that Jesus could do something for him. When the sisters sent word, Jesus did not go. Jesus' delay was deliberate. He picked the hour for the sign and the time for his approach. Similarly, he selected the time for his death, John 10:18 *No man taketh it from me, but I lay it down of myself. I have power to lay it down, and I have power to take it again. This commandment have I received of my Father.*

The Jews did not embalm but perfumed and buried the body on the day of death. Sometimes, even after burial, a comatose person might revive, "come back to life". The people believed the spirit of a person stayed near the body for three days and then departed.

Four days had passed since Lazarus had died. Martha and Mary felt grief, resentment and pain. Mary, Martha, and Lazarus were among Jesus' closest friends. Their home had been a haven for Him. They were disciples.

Jesus did not pray to the Father for power to raise Lazarus, nor did He ask the Father to do it. He prayed a prayer of thanksgiving, grateful that the

Father already had heard and answered Him. Lazarus' time had not yet come.

On Palm Sunday, Jesus entered the city of Jerusalem humbly riding,

John 12:14 *14 And Jesus, when he had found a young ass, sat thereon; as it is written.*

The crowd waved palm branches, the symbol of national unity and freedom. His Palm Sunday entrance, even without swords, confronted and challenged the religious community and the Roman Empire.

Jesus knew his hour had come –

John 13:1 *Now before the feast of the passover, when Jesus knew that his hour was come that he should depart out of this world unto the Father, having loved his own which were in the world, he loved them unto the end. His death was imminent. Earlier visits to Jerusalem had caused conflict, and the temple police had tried to arrest him.*

John 7:45-47 *45 Then came the officers to the chief priests and Pharisees; and they said unto them, why have ye not brought him?*

46 The officers answered, Never man spake like this man.

47 Then answered them the Pharisees, are ye also deceived? Jesus' raising of Lazarus resulted in many coming to believe in Him.

The disciples were confused, the crowds were recklessly exuberant, the authorities sensed political crisis, but Jesus used the moment to teach about his forthcoming death – what He called His hour of glory.

John 12:24 *24 Verily, verily, I say unto you, except a corn of wheat fall into the ground and die, it abideth alone: but if it die, it bringeth forth much fruit.*

Jesus could have toned down His message. Instead, He gave up His life in obedient self-sacrifice, dying to bring forth a rich harvest. Think how many people have been forgiven, how many children have been blessed, how many hungry have been fed by the "fruit" because Jesus, the single grain, fell into the earth. According to John's Gospel, Jesus' sacrificial death brings life abundant.

We recognize death as part of life. Even when someone we love dies; we do not grieve as those who have no hope. Our hope is in Jesus.

John 11:25 *Jesus said unto her, I am the resurrection, and the life: he that believeth in me, though he were dead, yet shall he live:*

Story 21

"Peacemakers"

In the Beatitudes in Matthew 5:9, Jesus said, *Blessed are the peacemakers: for they shall be called the children of God.*

I had a good friend in LaGrange, the Registrar at LHS who used to say, (at least a thousand times), "There are two kinds of people: Talkers and Doers". Having been in administration for a number of years, I made up my own saying. "There are two kinds of people – people who create problems and those who solve problems." By the nature of the job, principals and assistant principals must solve a lot of problems.

Another good friend in LaGrange was Assistant Director of Parks and Recreation for LaGrange and Troup County. I was in a Bible Study with him that met for nine years every Wednesday night. He was a great guy who would do anything for you. He would take the shirt off his back if you needed it. He was without a doubt the most sincere and helpful person that I have ever known. Unfortunately, at age thirty-eight, he found that he had melanoma and died two years later at the age of forty.

He was a great guy who only had one major fault. In athletics and athletic competition, he had an uncontrollable temper. We had some great football teams in LaGrange and some highly recruited athletes. In fact, at one time about ten years ago, we had four defensive backs starting in the pros. One year we had a linebacker who was highly recruited by all the major colleges. He narrowed his choice down to two colleges: Georgia and Clemson. Now he was a huge University of Georgia fan and got to know the recruiting coordinator at Georgia at that time. He was more than just active in recruiting our linebacker for Georgia. He thought that he had him committed to Georgia. Early in the morning on signing day the local radio station announced both our linebacker and our quarterback were going to sign with Clemson. I knew he was going to be furious with our head coach. Sure enough, right after we arrived at the office, he walked in. He was so mad his face was blood-red. He told our head coach, "Someone ought to knock your head off." Coach responded that if he was man enough to do it, then come on. He raced toward coach as I stepped between them pushing him with my hands and blocking coach with my big rear end. They were both swinging at each other before he finally left the building. They were both great friends of mine, and I was definitely a reluctant "peacemaker".

Any administrator serves as a "peacemaker" in breaking up fights between students, or arguments between teachers. However, in the Beatitudes and in other places in the Bible, Jesus is not referring to peace as the absence of conflict, but as the presence of God. According to the New Testament, peace results from God's forgiveness.

Philippians 4:7 *And the peace of God, which passeth all understanding, shall keep your hearts and minds through Christ Jesus.*

Peace is a mark of serenity to be sought after, and it summarizes the gospel message. It is a fruit of the Spirit; it will benefit those who practice it both now and at the Second Coming and is the opposite of disorder or confusion. The Christian who knows peace is charged to tell others, so that it may come for them, too, through Christ, who brought, preached, and is our peace.

Story 22

Grandchildren

Some years ago, I entered a new phase of my life (having grandchildren) which many of you entered long before me. I have two brothers and no sisters. I have two sons and no daughters. Now I have two granddaughters. You can imagine how I feel about them, and they love their granddaddy. We have a special relationship.

Sandra and I usually end up babysitting one or two days a week. When Ruthie was nine months old, Sandra and I were asked to keep her for eight days while my son and daughter-in-law took a well-deserved vacation to Aruba. They had saved up an abundance of frequent flyer miles from work that they needed to use. Six hours after they took off, we found out that my mother had passed away after having Alzheimer's for ten years.

Sandra and I packed up our nine-month-old granddaughter and headed to South Alabama. In a way it was a healthy diversion during a time of extreme grief for Sandra and me.

And you know, grandchildren can be a real delight and at other times really testing. Ruthie had a set time to go to bed at night, but she would really fight it. When she is at our house, I was the designated person to put her in the bed after Sandra gives her a bath. After reading her a couple of bedtime stories I rock her on my shoulder for a couple of minutes before putting her in the bed. One night I was telling her how much granddaddy loved her and she raised her head up, turned around and kissed me on the lips. Now that will touch you right in the heart.

At other times she is far from an angel. We keep her occasionally on weekends. She had just entered her terrible twos. When we say, "no" it means "yes" to her. When we say, "stop" it means "keep on" to her. She opens every drawer and every cabinet that she can reach. One Saturday we were keeping her, and she knows that turning off the TV is an automatic "time out" for her in the playpen. She turned the TV off not once, but five times, each time getting "time out" in her playpen in the dining room. Each "time out" lasted longer than the one before. When she thought that she had served her sentence long enough we could hear her saying, "Da diddy, I so sowwy".

My philosophy as a principal was: "Children will normally do what you expect them to do, if you communicate those expectations to them on a regular and consistent basis."

I also believe as a principal and disciplinarian that you could not discipline a child unless you cared for him or her. God teaches us the reverse: If you love your child you will discipline him or her.

The Bible also teaches us that we are mandated to teach our children about God and His love for us. We realize that our religion and Christianity are always just one generation away from extinction. That's scary!!!

Jesus has much to say about children in the Bible: Matthew 18:1-6

1 At the same time came the disciples unto Jesus, saying, Who is the greatest in the kingdom of heaven?

2 And Jesus called a little child unto him, and set him in the midst of them,

3 And said, Verily I say unto you, Except ye be converted, and become as little children, ye shall not enter into the kingdom of heaven.

4 Whosoever therefore shall humble himself as this little child, the same is greatest in the kingdom of heaven.

5 And whoso shall receive one such little child in my name receiveth me.

6 But whoso shall offend one of these little ones which believe in me, it were better for him that a millstone were hanged about his neck, and that he were drowned in the depth of the sea.

Mark 9:35-37
35 And he sat down, and called the twelve, and saith unto them, If any man desire to be first, the same shall be last of all, and servant of all.

36 And he took a child, and set him in the midst of them: and when he had taken him in his arms, he said unto them,

37 Whosoever shall receive one of such children in my name, receiveth me: and whosoever shall receive me, receiveth not me, but him that sent me.

Luke 18:15-17
15 And they brought unto him also infants, that he would touch them: but when his disciples saw it, they rebuked them.

16 But Jesus called them unto him, and said, Suffer little children to come unto me, and forbid them not: for of such is the kingdom of God.

17 Verily I say unto you, Whosoever shall not receive the kingdom of God as a little child shall in no wise enter therein.

Story 23

Jesus is the Key

If you looked closely at the old pants that I wore today you would see that the left pocket of my pants is worn out. You can probably all guess why. It's the pocket that I carry my keys in. When I was a principal, I had a huge set of keys – keys to every room or closet in the building. Before I moved to Rome in 1989 to become a principal, I was Assistant Principal at a Jr. High School in the morning and Athletic Director at LaGrange High School in the afternoon and nighttime. I had two big sets of keys. I soon learned the larger the set of keys you had, the more responsibility you had.

Keys come in all sizes and shapes and serve many purposes.

I recently went out of town with a good friend of mine. He told us that he and his wife made extra keys to their new car. When they tried to use them on several occasions, they opened the car, turned the ignition, but the car would not start. They learned that their original keys had a required computer chip in them and no key without their chip would start their car.

Today, we want to talk briefly about more important keys – the key to life, liberty, and love. Jesus is the key.

1) Jesus is the key to life.

John 3:36 - *He that believeth on the Son hath ever-lasting life: and he that believeth not the Son shall not see life; but the wrath of God abideth on him.*

Romans 6:23 - *For the wages of sin is death; but the gift of God is eternal life through Jesus Christ our Lord.*

1 John 5:11-12
11 And this is the record, that God hath given to us eternal life, and this life is in his Son.

12 He that hath the Son hath life; and he that hath not the Son of God hath not life.

2) Jesus is the key to Liberty
John 8:34-36
34 Jesus answered them, Verily, verily, I say unto you, Whosoever committeth sin is the servant of sin.

35 And the servant abideth not in the house for ever: but the Son abideth ever.

36 If the Son therefore shall make you free, ye shall be free indeed.

2 Corinthians 3:17 - *Now the Lord is that Spirit: and where the Spirit of the Lord is, there is liberty.*

3) Jesus is the key to Love: This is presented in Scriptures as the very nature of God-
1 John 4:8 - *He that loveth not knoweth not God; for God is love.*

1 John 4:16 - *And we have known and believed the love that God hath to us. God is love; and he that dwelleth in love dwelleth in God, and God in him.*

Love is also presented as the greatest of the Christian virtues – 1 Corinthians 13:13 - *And now abideth faith, hope, charity, these three; but the greatest of these is charity.*

Love found its supreme expression in the self-sacrifice on Calvary,

1 John 4:10 - *Herein is love, not that we loved God, but that he loved us, and sent his Son to be the propitiation for our sins.*

Jesus is the key to life liberty and love.

Story 24

Christian Limits

The Mississippi River begins as a tiny trickle of fresh water in northern Minnesota and sweeps down through the American plains as one of the largest rivers on earth. Running 2,470 miles to the Gulf of Mexico, it surges with industry, supplies drinking water to many communities, and serves as the watershed for middle America.

Its powerful currents are constrained by an elongated levee system that keeps the river within its banks, making it a productive channel of commerce. If the river had no banks, it would be useless.

The productive Christian is one whose life knows certain restraints. Although we are freed from the enslaving power of sin and death, we live within certain God-given limits.

Our limits are placed by God to deepen our spiritual life, not to suppress it.

Having worked in education for thirty-four years, I can assure you that young people want limits, even beg for limits, being placed on them by their parents and teachers. The best adjusted children are those that have strict, consistent limits placed on them. Children with the most problems are those that have no limits placed on them by their parents and limits are not enforced consistently. In the worst of all situations, children establish their own limits.

I remember a situation involving my wife who was a high school counselor at LaGrange High School. A mother came to her about her daughter whose grades were falling miserably. My wife asked what the problem was. The mother said that her daughter had her own private telephone in her room and stayed on the phone all night instead of doing her homework and studying. My wife said the solution was simple, "just disconnect the telephone and take it out of her room until her grades improve". Two weeks later the mother returned to my wife's office and said that her advice was a failure. My wife asked the mother if she had disconnected her daughter's private telephone. The mother replied, "Yes, but it didn't do any good – she just stayed on my phone all the time". Duh!!! In this case the daughter had recognized a void and had taken ownership of the family.

Just as the Mississippi River has limits determined by its levees and banks, we as Christians are given commandments in the Bible to govern our daily lives. The Bible makes it very clear that God is not satisfied with mere external compliance with his commandments but expects willing and joyful obedience, coming from the heart.

Story 25

Don't Look Back

Sandra and I were in the house one Saturday morning while our youngest son, Jason, was outside playing with the kids in the neighborhood. They were playing chase and Jason was the one being chased. All of a sudden, we heard a loud scream. Jason had looked back to see the chasing kids when he ran headfirst into a large white oak tree. Hours later we left the ER after Jason received several stitches in his forehead. LESSON: Don't look back.

I hesitate to tell this story, but since I am old and this happened nearly forty years ago, I guess I can confess. In 1980, I was named Athletic Director at LaGrange High School and one of the duties was to speak to the Rotary Club. The Rotary Club membership was all the "Big Wigs" in LaGrange: business leaders and owners; doctors; lawyers; pastors, and of course, my Superintendent of Schools. I was very apprehensive to say the least. Also, I was training for a 10K road race and ran five miles before work that morning and became dehydrated. I had prepared a good speech but the speaker (me) was a total disaster. I was sweating buckets and my hands were so nervous. I kept knocking things off the podium. I was very embarrassed. But I wouldn't let it end there. I kept looking back. For the next thirty years every time I was asked to speak in public (which was hundreds of times), my first thought was ROTARY CLUB 1980. It was embedded in my mind. I kept LOOKING BACK.

But God tells us not to look back. Remember Lot's wife? In Genesis 19:26 *But his wife looked back from behind him, and she became a pillar of salt.* She looked back to the earthly things instead of forward to God's plan for her life. Prior to God's destroying Sodom and Gomorrah, Abraham begged God to save the people. He argued until it was clear there was no one righteous.

In God's mercy, Abraham's nephew, Lot, and his family were allowed to leave, but He gave instructions to them not to look back. However, Lot's wife disobeyed and looked behind to see what she was leaving and was instantly turned into a pillar of salt. When we look back, we fail to see God's blessing for us in the future.

Philippians 3:13-14
13 Brethren, I count not myself to have apprehended: but this one thing I do, forgetting those things which are behind, and reaching forth unto those things which are before,

14 I press toward the mark for the prize of the high calling of God in Christ Jesus.

We need to look to a better future in Christ, rather than looking back to what we had in the past. Imagine trying to drive a car by using only the rearview mirror.

Genesis 19:17*And it came to pass, when they had brought them forth abroad, that he said, Escape for* *thy life; look not behind thee, neither stay thou in all the plain; escape to the mountain, lest thou be consumed.*

Again, Lot and his family were running for their lives and being told not to look back.

Luke 9:62 *And Jesus said unto him, No man, having put his hand to the plough, and looking back, is fit for the kingdom of God.*

Jesus is saying that in order to serve in His kingdom, you must give up your past and completely commit to serving Him in all your future actions and deeds.

Hebrews 10:38-39
38 Now the just shall live by faith: but if any man draw back, my soul shall have no pleasure in him.

39 But we are not of them who draw back unto perdition; but of them that believe to the saving of the soul.

Once we pledged our faith in Christ and Christ alone, He does not want us to Look BACK. We are all sinners and fall in sin but we are not to live in it. Christ died so we could be forgiven of our sins, but only if we confess and CHANGE our behavior and LOOK FORWARD.

About the Author

Jack spent 34 years in education, starting as a math teacher, a football, basketball, baseball coach, and athletic director at a large high school. He was also a boy's Junior High School Assistant Principal, Junior High School Principal, and Elementary School Principal.

He has been married to his wife, Sandra, for 54 years, and they have two sons, Jeff and Jason. They have two granddaughters, Ruth and Rachel.

He has been a member of the Methodist church all of his life. He has served in leadership positions at every level. He has been an elementary Sunday

School teacher, adult teacher, and senior adult teacher.

Jack attended the University of Alabama, Troy University, LaGrange College, Georgia Southern University, and the University of West Georgia. He has a B.A. degree and a master's degree in math and add-on master's degree in Educational Leadership as well as an Educational Specialist (six-year) degree in administration and supervision.

He is a full-time caregiver for his wife, Sandra, who has had Multiple Sclerosis for twenty years and is in a wheelchair. She is a retired English teacher and high school counselor.

Jack's passion is golf, but he loves to exercise. He either plays golf, walks a five-mile trek in the neighborhood, or goes to the fitness center every day but Sunday, when he gives his 77-year-old legs a rest.